I don't really know much about life but the best thing one can get out of life is passive income and I know you are reading this because you want this same thing. Think of the voice reading this right now as a voice from the dust ready to guide you to achieving your goal. Knowledge is key to success and you don't need to have a PhD to be able to afford your first house come on, you don't need to work 12hours job every day and can't still afford a Lamborghini for yourself.

Have you thought about when you are 70, who is going to do all the work for you? Am pleading with you to try all you can now at whatever age you are right now to provide a future that you and your family would be proud of.

Visit my page to view all possible means you can build a future for yourself ()

"Learning never stops" Cheers!!!

CONTENT

INTRODUCTION

Time Time Time, I think it's time for us to talk about time. Its sounds funny but we don't have to be all serious you know.

For you to be able to accomplish time management which am going to share in this book, you have to be willing to do something.......... You need to be willing to let go of the past, yes you need to.

Remember the thousands of dollars you lost to Facebook ads, or to online scams or to affiliate marketing or to bitcoin or to whatever you might have lost money on, that's a lot of dollars but thinking about them will only accumulate fear in you and keep you in the past.

Living in the past does not only involve the money you have lost, sometimes it also involves people who has left your life like your girlfriend broke up with you or you dad sent you out of the house or your mum is very ill or you lost your dad. I mean whatever has happened to you, you need to be willing to let all of those go before we can continue to the next level. The reason this is important is because nobody has time so you need to create it and if you can clear your recycle bin right now, I think you know what I mean, you will have more time to focus on more productive things.

TIME

I really don't know how to define time but I feel it's that tic tic tic sound that comes from the clock in your living room. It's honestly the truth, and the other half of the truth is that that sound means something different to everybody. Take for example Bill Gates, yea the popular guy makes $114.16 every tic sound for being alive, that's quite big right. Think about Mark Zuckerberg, the Facebook guy makes $46.30 per tic. Those are amazing people with amazing things happening around them, you don't have to be them but you still need to understand how time works and ask yourself what does a minute mean to me or what does the tic sound mean to me. When you have found out what time means to you, then you have to set a goal on what you want time should be for you because I have this strong feeling that God will ask us how well we used the time he gave to us.

But there is one enemy I know of time which is laziness so am going to help you understand how to handle it so it won't ruin everything.

Think about moments you said this;

"Today I don't feel like doing anything

I just wanna lay in my bed.

Don't feel like picking up my phone.

So leave a message at the tone

Cause today I swear I'm not doing anything

Uh, I'm gonna kick my feet up and stare at the fan

Turn the TV on

Throw my hand in my pants

Nobody's gon' tell me I can't"

Bruno Mars right! But that guy already made it and he can choose to be lazy but you can't afford to be lazy because you going to lose a lot so when next you feel lazy, try the following;

BREAKDOWN TASK INTO SMALLER TASKS

When a task looks big, overwhelming or intimidate, I don't know if there is an hormone that just naturally starts to secret that lazy feeling and before you know it, you skip the task, procrastinate or wake up the next 5hrs magically.

Breaking a task into pieces makes it look less overwhelming and easier to handle so you need to try that out.

DON'T SKIP SLEEP AND EXERCISES

Sometimes you might feel you are doing a good job by skipping sleep at night while you know you have a task to do the next day and when the time comes to work, you start having the lazy feeling.

Don't skip your night rest for anything, even if it's to make love or whatever, just plan a better time to do that.

Always exercise when you rise from bed no matter how small it is, it will help drive laziness to some distance

I know a friend in Australia who will way to where they have expensive glass houses for sale, take a walk around, asks for the price of the houses (which obviously would be huge) then gets enough motivation to rush back home and make more money because he wants a good house to live in with his family.

You also need to look for something that's going to keep you motivated and keep you on track, if you can do this, laziness will shy away

HAVE A VISION OF WHAT YOU WANT TO BE

Having a perfect picture of what you want to be in the next few months can also be the drive you need to catapult you out of the world of laziness,

THINK ABOUT BENEFITS AND CONSEQUENCES

Yes, what you have to gain if you work and what you have to lose has to be on your mind. If I know that going out there for 3hrs will earn me $150 and lazing around the home will earn me nothing, I think I would rather be running to work, you get the idea right? Ok.

AVOID PROCASTINATION

I don't know if you have been doing this but don't do it again and if you have never procrastinated, please don't try it. It's a total waste of time so never fall victim of this.

So now that you are able to handle laziness, let's move on

If you have ever made that mistake or if you are still making it that goals and plans are the same, then you need to change that way of thinking because they are totally different. Goal is that destination you desire to reach so it's more like the end game while the plan is what you have to do to arrive that destination or particular goal you already set for yourself. They both require the same require the same amount of preparation so don't think that planning takes a lot more time that setting of goals. If a goal is properly set then the plan to bring it into realization won't be that difficult to put up. So keep in mind that whenever you write down a goal, a plan needs to be drawn up immediately to aid to the goal and all this must be realistic (achievable)

The best thing about making a plan for a goal you have set is that you will come to realize tiny goals that you have to incorporate in your plan in other to achieve that ultimate goal you have set. Quick case study below;

Goal

- *I want to start an ecommerce store*

Plan

- *Save money for the hosting of the store (sub-goal A)*
- *Buy a theme and a domain*
- *Learn little coding to enable me to edit the theme to fit the store without hiring someone (sub-goal B)*

Sub-goal A

- *Buy hosting for the store*

Plan

- *Get a job*
- *Spend less money (cut coffee and movies)*

Sub-goal B

- *Learn little coding*

Plan

- *Spend more time downloading YouTube tutorials and watching*
- *Meet James whole is a programmer for some tips......*

And that's how the plan to get an ecommerce store goes on and on, so writing out the plan really makes it easier to know what you want to do and what stage you are currently in.

How to Set Goals

Goals reflect the desires of our hearts and our vision of what we want to accomplish. Through goals and plans, our hopes are transformed into action.

Set goals for each key indicator that will be explained on the next page. You may also set goals for your personal development. Do all you can to achieve your goals on daily and weekly interval. The ultimate measure of success is not in achieving goals alone but in the service you render and the progress of others.

"I am so thoroughly convinced that if we don't set goals in our life and learn how to master the techniques of living to reach our goals, we can reach a ripe old age and look back on our life only to see that we reached but a small part of our full potential. When one learns to master the principles of setting a goal, he will then be able to make a great difference in the results he attains in this life."

—President M. Russell Ballard. Talk given to Salt Lake Area young adults, Oct. 18, 1981

Specific Goals

Don't you ever be like 'today, am going to learn something new' or 'am going to be better than I was yesterday' without fist writing down specifically what you want to learn or become better at.

Imagine the human brain wakes up with maximum power of 100% to use for the day. Taking away miscellaneous (chores, gym, etc...), you are left with approximately 70% power for the day. Consider the following;

Study 1

I decided to go about my day that am going to learn something new, then I try to understand that comes my way in the name of learning, saw my friend building a website and decided to sit with him to see if I can pick up some things, after much time, got bored and left for an open space to clear my head. While taking some air, a friend dropped by and we started this gist about girls which took a while, we had lunch together and when he left, I went online to do some chatting and that was it. 24 hours gone gaining nothing, learning nothing but am tired and exhausted but I don't feel fulfilled for the day.

I woke up with a plan to learn how to build a blog, so in the morning, I started by looking up some books on kindle, then called a friend who lives across town and has a reputable blog to set up a meeting for lunch. Studied all morning and had lunch with this friend who gave me all the tips I needed. At the end of the day, I was able to get the knowledge I wanted because it was specific goal. I build my blog the next day and you can check out a book I wrote on how to build your own blog on my page

I know you might have heard of planning severally but we will do something different which is using key indicators. Let's briefly look at the key indicators;

- Goal set
- Goal achieved
- Knowledge gained
- Time (Its constant, either a day or 7days)

The key indicators work differently and are used at different times for measuring performance so you have to use them right.

Now that we know the key indicators lets learn about planning

DAILY planning

Your day will end up more productive if you plan it a night before, it's going to help you capture all the events for the day. To better help you understand how to go about daily planning, let's make a case study.

Goal set; I at 9pm picks up my planner and arrange the activities for the day as usual, I then right down things I want to achieve during the day (for example make $20 extra or building a website)

Knowledge; I need to know something new tomorrow for me to actually maximize my potential so I will write down (how to fix an hard drive)

Time; 24hrs

Then I go to bed............ 24hrs later

* I check if Goal achieved 100%, if yes, then time was used well and set new goals and if no, goals will be carried over alongside new goals
* I also check Knowledge gained; have I leant something new today, if yes then time was used well but if no, you will have this empty feeling if you actually put your mind to it and you will want to improve the next day
* Then you go on to make the plan for the next day

It might seem difficult to start this process but if you can do iy trice, you will get used to it and buy the 5th time you do it, you will find yourself a whole new person

WEEKLY planning

This is a broader version of the daily plan. It's done once a week on a day preferable by you, and its captures goals you have for the next seven days.

Note that the goals you set in your daily planning are taking from the bunch of goals in you plan for the week.

MESURING performance

Measuring performance is the most important part of panning.

> "When performance is measured, performance improves. When performance is measured and reported, the rate of improvement accelerates."
>
> –President Thomas S. Monson. "Thou Art a Teacher Come from God," Improvement Era, Dec. 1970, 101

I really love those amazing words from president Monson. Always compare your goals and actuals to measure you growth so your level of improvement can be accelerated.

The key indicators revealed in this book were given to help you pattern your life towards steady growth so it is necessary that you set goals according to the indicators. This might sound new or different from the way you have probably been doing things but you have to be willing to try this new method.

There is a saying that *"only a fool will keep doing one thing the same way and expecting a different result"*. You don't have to be that person. Right here and now, you need to be willing to let go of things that don't bring results, if you have been trying one particular thing in a particular way, you have to stop it as it will only result in greater pain, money loss and wasted time.

 You also need to be willing to let go of things that doesn't bring you joy, I mean things that you do but aren't happy about. The reason you have to do this is because you won't be able to make the best out of it even if others around you are making it.

Allow Time for Distraction

All work and no play makes jack a dull boy right? **While working for** long hours to achieve your goal stress will definitely build up and you can't sometimes clear your head with a chat, sometimes you need to really get distracted, play like a child, have a cold drink, treat yourself like a king or queen that you are, do a little crazy stuff, always add this to your plan whenever you notice fatigue or stress.

Think of that moment you hit that F5 key to refresh your pc, that's the feeling you need to get after this exercise. After practicing this, your body will come alive and by the time you get back to work, you will be amazing

When you try the formula in this book for a few days, you will definitely start to see some difference in your lifestyle and I know you will then start looking for shortcuts for example skipping daily and weekly planning sessions, but that's a really bad idea. Never skip sessions even when you are tired because every day you skip a session, you automatically fall in productivity and your drop might be faster than expected.

Don't throw away those books you wrote your goals and plans as you will need them in the future for reference purpose.

Stretch

Goals you set has to be such that they help you stretch beyond your normal ability, so don't set goals that are too comfortable. Try as much to set all goals in line with that grand dream you have on your mind somewhere so you won't fall off track. Stretching in goal setting improves the rate of growth faster than you can imagine.

Yes, we all want to get there, we all want to be perfect at what we do but you shouldn't force it, let it come normally as you continue to practice the basic steps involved in achieving your goal.

Sometimes you might feel rushing the process will get things done quicker which is really true, but will it add any value to you? Would you have grown? The answer is No and No so don't see rushing as an option.

You need to be accountable to someone, I strictly suggest a mentor (someone you trust) but if no one is available then you have to accountable to yourself. Accountability to oneself is really difficult as you might be too loose to yourself or might be too strict but either ways there must be a judge to help you out and if that judge is you, be honest with yourself in al that you do.

Finally, in everything you do, always remember to pray, it's the truth.

REMEMBER THE FOLLOWING

- ❖ Set specific Goals (What needs to be done?)

- ❖ Set goals according to the key indicators.

- ❖ For each key indicator, set goals that help you stretch and work effectively.

- ❖ Conduct weekly and daily planning sessions

- ❖ Keep a daily and weekly planner.

- ❖ Focus your efforts on your purpose.

- ❖ Allow **time** for distractions.

- ❖ Pray mightily over your goals and plans.

- ❖ Always account for your efforts

- ❖ Resist the urge the rush

- ❖ Don't force perfection, let it come naturally

- ❖ Stop doing things that don't bring joy or result

- ❖ Let go of the past

- ❖ Respond/engage only when you are ready

And that's it's for time mastery, don't forget to leave a positive review. I love you and hope to see you succeed.

Find more books on my page; Marcus Osaz

Feel free to send me an email on what you were able to achieve with this book; Myboy1997@gmail.com

www.ingramcontent.com/pod-product-compliance
Lightning Source LLC
Chambersburg PA
CBHW070937220526

45468CB00005B/1811